Copyrighted Mate

GW01315998

How to Dress For your Shape
Fuller Body Type

Copyrighted Material

How to Dress For your Shape
Fuller Body Type

By Isabella James

Copyrighted Material

First published by INFORMOTIONS LLC

Kindle Edition 2012

Copyright © Isabella James 2012

ISBN-13: 978-1494344955

ISBN-10: 1494344955

Trade Paperback 2013

All rights reserved. No part of this publication may be reproduced in any form or by any means without the permission of the publisher.

INFORMOTIONS LLC, PO BOX 17501, WILMINGTON, DE 19803

Copyrighted Material

Contents:

Copyrighted Material

Welcome

Dear Readers, I have created this guide for women of all shapes and sizes. The book is available in four versions Average, Fuller, Petite and Tall body types. There is some common text and lessons between all the guides with advice that's of value to all women. The critical section Catalog of Fashion Choices also known as "The Guide" contains over 110 illustrations with advice for your specific body type and is unique to a fuller sized body type. Truly that advice is at the heart of this guide and was a tremendous labor of love to develop this book. I hope you come along for the ride and welcome your feedback at our website Dressity.com while you are there sign up for our newsletter so we can stay in touch, no worries I never spam and I never sell list.

Copyrighted Material

Introduction: Being Stylish Over Fashionable

Welcome to your personalized style guide! I am so excited that you have chosen to take the first and most important step into your new, more confident future. In the following pages, I will teach you how to choose clothes that suit your individual body shape. Once you see what a difference a few small changes can make to your confidence, you will know that your new wardrobe showcases your body in the best possible light. You will be more relaxed and free to be yourself or the person you have always hoped to be.

I have designed this book to be the simplest and most thorough style guide you can find. Over the years, I have amassed a large knowledge base coupled with real world experience as a professional stylist and here I will share with you the same styling tips that I reserve for my clients. Having seen these tools make such a difference in women's lives, I can honestly say that the skills you will learn from this book will make you think differently about clothes for the rest of your life.

I have been very careful to explain everything clearly and concisely, allowing you to soak up the information quickly to use while shopping and dressing. I have also included "Closet Exercises" at the end of the first three chapters that will create a more organized approach to your new image. If carried out in order, you will achieve an immaculate closet that matches your flawless wardrobe. Lastly, you will find an Index filled with illustrations that portray the types of clothes that you as an fuller shaped woman should prioritize. And because fashion is such an evolving force, I have stripped away information that is too trend oriented. That way, this book and the skills you will learn within will be something you can use for many years to come.

Working behind the scenes in the fashion industry has shown me the true nature of the beast, and I have learned a lot about femininity and self esteem, and I want to pass it on to you

Copyrighted Material

in hopes that it will empower you. Whenever you feel insecure about the way you look, and we all do at times, re-read these parts to remind yourself that the industry is not in the business of portraying reality.

In the fashion industry, there is a large emphasis on being fashionable; this means creating a want for all the latest trends. A person who considers themselves fashionable wants to be seen in the most up-to-date pieces at all times, and commonly will only wear an outfit once. They will talk in riddles about what is 'in' or 'out' and see their own clothes as the 'must have' items of the season. They are constantly looking ahead to what is next, and are often on waiting lists for various designer items. These women may even judge others harshly for not having the latest bag, or most recent design. Their confidence is only achieved once they have all the 'right' clothes on, but next season everything must be thrown out and the process starts all over again.

Conversely, someone who is stylish does not need to be a part of an exclusive club. They appreciate clothes as extensions of themselves that show the world who they are. They find no need to judge others and will openly compliment another woman for her fashion sense. They know what suits them and are not dictated by the whims of the fashion world, but will just as happily jump for joy as new styles hit the shops. A stylish woman already has the confidence to enjoy who they are and how they look. Her wardrobe will be a selection of clothes that fit well and have stood the test of time, yet also be intermingled with a few high fashion pieces that are fun to wear.

The most important piece of advice that I can give you is this: Wear clothes that celebrate your strengths and play down your weaknesses. This is done by being critical about what fashion has to offer each season and whether it will work for you. In the real world, it just makes sense to create a stylish wardrobe that lasts, over a fashionable one. There are many arguments about style and whether it can be bought or learned, but I see gobs of rich women with zero style, and plenty of women that always

Copyrighted Material

seem to look good with a limited budget. Most telling is someone who has understood what looks good on them and wears clothing that suits their body shape and size. In this book, I will teach you how to select the styles you need to create the right balance for your body. Style will be what women notice about you, and it will soon be something you do effortlessly every day.

After you read this book, I know that you will revolutionize your image. Thinking about how clothes work and the qualities they can bring to your body and life will surprise you. This is information that you will use for the rest of your days.

Breaking Your Misconceptions

Over the years I have worked with many women, just like you, who were looking for a way to change their look and create an image that better reflects who they are. One of the reasons it is so difficult is because the way we feel about ourselves and our bodies is constantly being manipulated by the media. We are inundated with commercials and print ads that force us to think about dieting, toning, looking younger or just looking better. And of course, each one has a beautiful woman in it looking effortlessly amazing. As a result, many women end up at odds with their bodies and scrutinize their every imperfection.

One would think that the beautiful women in the magazines have a wonderful life, but as a model are they happier with their bodies than average women? We see them artfully made up and adorned in the most exquisite designer fashions, and photographed in the most sophisticated settings; it's easy to believe that they have it all, and therefore must be fulfilled and content. The fact is, after all the clothes are taken off, the hair dismantled and the makeup removed, they feel the same as you and I. Like us, they have good days and bad. They struggle with bills and worry about what will come at them next. Relationships are just as challenging for them because honesty and respect don't

Copyrighted Material

become easier to find just because you model clothes for a living. The difference between them and us is that we don't have our imperfections pointed out to us on a daily basis by casting directors and designers. All day long, they are told what is wrong with their bodies; their imperfections are constantly on blast. Sooner or later, they all begin to feel the pressure, and they too will blame their thick ankles or curvy hips for obstructing their happiness.

A recent study, conducted by a top American fashion magazine, surveyed over 5000 women and found that nearly 70% of them did not like the way their body looked. Nearly 50% of the women studied were currently on a weight loss plan, with some even using laxatives and/or fasting. I also receive numerous emails everyday from women all over the country, begging me to help them hide their flaws and many express their desperation to become slimmer, curvier, or more toned, often using a model or print ad as a reference. Unfortunately, our relationship with ourselves can be very confusing and it is easy to fantasize when we look at these pictures, that because a model appears happy or confident on the page, then their physical perfection is the key to their happiness. Always keep in mind that they are being paid to smile and all the clothes they are wearing are pinned up in the back to appear to fit perfectly. Being happy with who you are and comfortable in your own skin is the key to happiness. Clothes will only be the first step on this journey, but knowing that you have chosen designs and shapes that help you look your very best will leave you free to concentrate on creating new relationships built on honesty and respect, making it easier for you to be respectful to yourself and boosting your confidence.

As we move forward, there are some key points I often review with each of my clients that I will list for you here. Each, in their own right, is important and should you need to re-read them from time to time I have confidence that you will feel rejuvenated and ready for whatever fashion trials lay ahead.

First of all, there is no such thing as a perfect body. Every grown woman has cellulite, a round tummy and uneven breasts—even

Copyrighted Material

models. Remind yourself of this against the fashion industry's milieu of post adolescent femininity so provocatively portrayed in print.

Hailing a cab, chasing down a bus, and just sitting down are all things we do during a normal day, but I am still waiting to see a fully styled model complete any of these mundane tasks safely on a runway, let alone on the street.

You are not more attractive because you're in pain. High heels, tight clothes and hair that looks like it was glued to the scalp may appear as high fashion, but these extras take only a moment to capture on film. After a shoot, all models remove the painful shoes, uncomfortable dresses and wash their hair before putting on running shoes and yoga pants to go home. That's what I wear to write pieces like this, and no matter what is said in the latest issue of Vogue, you can too.

The phrase "Plus Size" is an appalling term, and all by itself has traumatized generations of curvy women. A size is just a size, no matter how high the numbers go. The average size of the American woman is 14, and I do not understand where "average" suddenly became "plus."

Before a big red carpet event, you can't find a pair of Spanx in a 200 mile radius around Los Angeles. Yes, even the most beautiful of celebrities wear intricate support under garments under their thin silk dresses. If you knew you were on your way to be judged, assessed, scrutinized, condemned and crucified in front of millions of people, you would too.

Lastly, don't forget that the beautiful woman who earns her living smiling for the camera is tragically preoccupied with her own imperfections as she struggles to represent the feminine ideal. After being told that her thighs are too thick, or her teeth too crooked she will make herself miserable trying to get a job that only the promise of a healthy paycheck will bring a fleeting smile to her face.

The best accessory you can wear will be your acceptance of your own body. Whatever its shape, it is yours, and it is doing its best

10

Copyrighted Material

everyday to support you through the myriad of surreptitious functions it performs without you ever thinking about them. Sadly, many of us forget this and lose touch with the fact that our bodies are more than just something we cover up. And being average is not always easy, but it need not dictate your image. I think many of you are subconsciously influenced by this adjective more than you realize, and here are a few key areas I think may have been impacted by it. For one, you probably enjoy dressing in layers to cover up the areas you feel are less than attractive. You most likely haven't been fitted for a bra in many years and would rather continue "guessing" at the smaller cup size than the one you suspect you need. Also, though you enjoy bright colors, you don't really know how to where pattern well. Lastly, you have mixed feelings about fashion. Usually, you like the latest styles, but only on a model because you feel that a real woman could never wear them. I have worked with a lot of women who love clothes and have a closet full, but they never wear anything that makes them feel confident and comfortable. It's important to realize that you don't have to compromise!

Further on in the book we will discuss your shape in more detail and I have some tricks that will help to flatter your individual silhouette. You will also find many styles that you will be able to prioritize in your wardrobe with the knowledge that what you wear flatters your curves. Use them to be all that you can be to yourself and to others!

Now, that is all I will say about the seedy underbelly of advertising and the fashion industry. We have all heard it before, and though we know that the photos we see have been airbrushed, they still can make us feel like we will never be good enough. So, let's push forward, because soon your new image and confidence will be all the armor you will need to defend against those feelings.

I believe that styling is one part know-how and two parts clothes counseling. We all have our insecurities and comfort zones, and each of us has our own set of unspoken "rules" that we follow as we shop and dress. I have yet to meet a woman that does not have

11

Copyrighted Material

a set of ideas already in place that determine their everyday style. I have often been told, 'I am too big for that!' or 'I don't have the body to pull that off!' These, and many other rules we create for ourselves need to be gently challenged, because they can be obstructive. Ask yourself if you really need them or are you just trying to protect yourself from the unknown? Changing the way you dress to something you wouldn't normally wear can be an emotional experience; perhaps that is what you are trying to avoid.

I have worked with a multitude of different types of women. The majority of them have all had a set idea about their style and/or body before they even set foot into my workshop. And though I may agree with some, others I try to change, mainly because they are based on outdated concepts they have about themselves. Now, let's go through some of the more common "rules" I get from my clients. Do you recognize any?

"I don't want to look as though I am trying too hard." Although some women put an extraordinary amount of effort into their appearance, the work doesn't always pay off because they don't know the basics. But after reading this book you won't have that problem. No matter the statement you are trying to make, your style choices will always look effortless.

"I only wear casual clothes" If you have adopted this rule, it may because you have lost confidence in your ability to pull off a structured look or maybe it is an idea you hide behind because you don't really know what to choose to flatter your average shape. Don't get me wrong, casual wear is great for downtime, but it is usually shapeless and dull. Is this how you want to the world to see you? More importantly, is this how you see yourself?

"I don't do girly." This usually means that you prefer a more dramatic, androgynous look, which is good; it means you have a signature style. If, however, this means you avoid skirts, floral prints, pastel colors and frilly tops, then you are missing out on a lot of fun! Now, it doesn't mean that you have to become an attention seeking hussy by celebrating your femininity with a

Copyrighted Material

little bit of color and skin, but try to push yourself out of your comfort zone slowly. Maybe just try a skirt with a t-shirt and a pair of light strappy sandals. Once you have tried this and worn it a few times, you will begin to try other more adventurous pieces.

"I'm much too old to pull that off." If this means that because you are getting older, you avoid certain styles that show too much skin, or take the time to plan out key pieces that have a certain quality to them or are well made, then you are on the right track. Conversely, if you just don't want to wear anything colorful, playful or trendy then I believe that you're presuming that getting older means that you have to become invisible. There is truly something to be said about a pinch of trend to reinvigorate a drab look.

"I only wear pants." I mainly hear this from concerned women who feel that their legs are so ugly that they should never see the light of day. If this is the case, then I suggest you peruse the skirt section of the illustration index to find the correct length, hem and shape to either disguise or hide the parts of your legs that you feel uncomfortable with. But maybe you just get caught up in the 'unsuitable shoe' trap, which inevitably happens every time you even think of wearing something other than pants. This is easy to fix, though. In all likelihood, all your shoes are intended to be worn with pants, so look for shoes that can work either way. If you are going to step out in a new skirt, you should splurge on a new pair of stems as well.

"I don't want anyone to see the tops of my arms." / "My stomach is too big for that top." These comments and others like it just mean that you would enjoy covering up in layers of fabric and hope that no one will see the shape underneath. This commonly happens when you focus too much on what you don't like about your body rather than what you do like about it and highlighting those areas. Make a list right now, of all your good points and use it as a reminder of all the things you want to showcase and then use the tips in this book to minimize or camouflage the others.

I get a lot of emails from women I work with that express their

Copyrighted Material

frustrations with the ever changing ideas and designs in the fashion industry. Just when you seem to have found something that suits you, it changes, and you can't be sure you will ever find it again. Similarly, fashion magazines and how-to experts often talk in seasons, what is perfectly acceptable one season is out the next. I don't know any other industry that operates this way, yet we receive it into our lives on that very basis. Of course, change is always good and making a change that feels right can be liberating.

Closet Exercise #1: Creating Your Signature Style

Whether we like it or not, people read us through our clothing. Without saying a single word, our outfit, hair and makeup choices speak volumes about who we are. People will even make assumptions about your personality based on your choices in color, design and print. All these things can affect the impression you make on potential friends, bosses, work colleagues or other social acquaintances. Now think about what you wear most often. Are all these people making the right assumptions about you? What words come to mind when you think about your wardrobe? My guess is that among your descriptions are words like "comfortable," "practical," or maybe even "old," "boring," and "bland."

I once worked with a woman who had an attachment to drab, colorless clothing, shapeless shirts and unkempt hair. She was surprised at how easily I recognized her lack of self-worth. I told her that I could immediately see that she no longer loved herself. She broke down and admitted that she just wore clothes without thinking, and she was just uninterested in the woman she saw in the mirror. You may have felt this way at one time or another, but soon you will be on the road to falling in love with you again.

Now remember, a stylish woman always communicates a regard for herself, and flaunts that she is comfortable in her own skin. People will make assumption s about a stylish woman that will include "thoughtful," "inspired," and "effortless." Lucky for us, these traits are fairly simply to imitate. The first step is to create a "Style Vision Board." I know that it may sound silly, or

14

Copyrighted Material

overdone, but surrounding yourself with inspiration and a visual representation of what you want your style to be and what you want your clothes to say about who you are will empower you to radiate a confidence that is truly lovely to be around. Your wardrobe will soon be full of thoughtfully chosen garments that will show off the best possible you.

Creating a "Style Vision Board" is fairly simple. You will need a large poster board for this project, and I suggest that the finished board be hung on the inside of your closet door; so, if you need to cut it to fit, I would do that first. If your board is already the desired size, you can begin filling your board with aspirational images and words that portray the kind of style you hope to achieve.

On the left side of the board, draw a line about two inches from the edge. Here you will fill the space with a list of adjectives. These descriptions will embody what you want your style to be and what you want people to assume about you based on your look. These could be descriptions or feelings like, "colorful," "coordinated," "smart," "sassy," "sophisticated," "glamorous," or even just "happy," "fun," "fresh-faced," or "natural." Keep it simple, and most importantly, realistic. Don't go so far away from your current style that the style you aspire to becomes so far-fetched that you feel it is unachievable.

Scan the internet or old magazines for images that represent how you wish your style to be. I suggest starting with celebrities whom you admire style-wise. Two of my favorite inspirations are Michelle Obama and Sarah Jessica Parker; one for my practical side and the other for my more funky side.

Now add shapes, colors and prints you like. They can be subtle or bold; modern or vintage; and even large or small weight. Arrange each one attractively on the board, while being mindful to avoid looks that are trend-oriented. Fads come and go, but the object here is to create a personal mood board that will last your for many years to come.

Once your vision board is complete, affix it to the inside of your

Copyrighted Material

closet door or anywhere else where it will remind you of your personal style signature. After all, the reason stylists seem to make such effortless choices is because they are constantly surrounded by clothes, models and designers and we are thinking about image and inspiration for the large part of the day. I am not saying that you should spend any longer than necessary on your image, but give yourself the opportunity to be inspired when you open your closet door in the morning.

These steps that I have outlined for you here are important, but so is thinking of yourself as unique and therefore, special. If you like a certain color, or want to dress in a certain way—go for it! Embrace it! Enjoy it! I don't subscribe to the idea that everyone should look the same. In fact, I feel very strongly that a stylish approach allows room for individuality. This honesty that you will have with yourself will shine through in your happiness and will show others that you are resplendent in your confidence.

It is also important that the signature style you create, outlives any trend or fashion fad, because your style is the thing that others will describe you by. It will influence the types of clothes that you buy, and fashion trends only last for a short period of time. This is where you take ownership of your look. Don't hand this power over to the fashion industry. It's the power to decide how you appear to the world.

Know Your Body Symmetry

Many people hear me say "Know your body symmetry," and think "What on Earth does that mean?" Well, for an average shaped person like you, it means you are all in proportion. Lucky you! You don't have to exert extra energy trying to even out your top half to your bottom half, or vice versa. With such a standard shape, there isn't much to learn about body symmetry, but maybe your upper arms are thicker than you would like, or perhaps you want to appear taller and more elegant. Whatever style you pursue, I want you to enjoy and revel in your beautiful and healthy body from this day forward. And you must endeavor to show off your curves to their best light.

16

Copyrighted Material

To emphasize your figure, you will need to define your bosom and hips allowing focus to shift to the smallest part of your waist, thus creating the ever-sought-after 'hourglass figure'. It is important to not get caught up in the size of a garment when looking for these qualities. This is mainly because there is no standardized sizing in the market; one store's 12 is the next store's 14. Fit is the key, and really the only thing that matters at this time. So stick to a shop or label that fits you best. A well-fitted garment doesn't have to cost a fortune either. The cheapest of garments can look amazing if fitted properly, and conversely, the most expensive outfit can cause a very negative impact if fitted badly. Here are a few dos and don'ts to keep in mind while checking the fit of new or old clothes.

Steer clear of boxy shapes like T-shirts or polo shirts. They hide your breasts and hips, making you look bulky and square.

Beware of high, round necklines that make your bosom appear saggy and unsupported.

Never wear Lycra that is too tight. This fabric can cling to fleshy areas making them appear lumpy or roll-like.

Avoid tops that blouse out at the hips. You will lose your waist and leave your body with no shape.

Remember to skip the lacy bra when wearing smooth fabrics like jersey. It makes your chest look mottled and sickly.

Choose gently fitted tops that are not skin tight. These will make your body seem streamlined and shapely. I advise you look for fitted shirts and blouses, or silky tops that create sheen, as well as shadow in some places. You can also look for Bohemian styles that are shaped to fit to your body.

If torn between a garment that accentuates your bosom or one that defines your waist, choose the waist defining garment first. This look will make the most of your curves.

Most average women still wish they had a fuller chest area. If this is you, look for tops that add volume to the area. Usually, you will see ruffles, pleats, or ruching of fabric in the front; all of

17

Copyrighted Material

which create the illusion of fullness.

Head towards V-necks to lengthen the neck and create a flattering line to your décolletage.

Make sure you have a properly fitted and smooth bra. It is crucial that you take the time to get the right fit, and that the straps do not cut into the flesh of your shoulder creating a lumpy affect. Also, breasts that point down or are spread outward are very ageing, so you want to make sure you get the appropriate amount of lift.

Wear large chunky knits only if they wrap around your frame seductively and accentuate your waist.

If you want to play down full shoulders and upper arms, look for wide shoulder straps, sweetheart necklines and 3-quarter length sleeves with flair.

Trousers and skirts are great tools for giving the illusion of length, but if your shape is slightly pear, as many petite and average sized women are, remember to choose bottoms that slightly flare from the hips so that your bum is not your widest point.

Enjoy a nice fitted pair of jeans as they will give your thighs a smooth and toned appearance.

Always wear a low heel under your slacks. I say this because high heels are just plain painful for most of us. Plus, "sophisticated cool" is not usually worn on the face of someone whose feet are in distress.

To visually make your legs appear longer, find a shoe that tonally matches your skirt or pants.

Skirts or capri pants that hover right around the knee are also fantastic for lengthening the leg. An A-line, knee-length skirt will flatter full calves and remember to pair with a low heel, but avoid any with an ankle strap as they will appear to "chop off" the leg.

Now that we have covered a few rules for dressing to create body symmetry, you must ask yourself these questions when deciding on a garment or style: "Does it fit?" "Does it give the look of

Copyrighted Material

quality?" "Do they appear cared for?" And most importantly, "Does it flatter your body?" Does it enhance your strengths and disguise your weaknesses?" If the item does none of these things; it does not belong on your body.

Closet Exercise #2: Clean Out!

It's time to use your new skills to clean out your current closet. It's important for you to see your clothes as tools for your new image, and your closet is your toolbox. Any mechanic will tell you that the secret to efficient work is a tidy toolbox, and for a stylist the same is true. For you to create the style that you envision you will need to see all the tools at your disposal.

Now, I am sure you are picturing your closet with all its badly hung clothing squished into one tiny space. There are probably hangers poking through sweaters, clothes on the floor, and many of its contents aren't even the right size. Am I right? Have no fear, you're not alone. Most women only wear one-third of their clothes and the rest is just clutter.

An excellent stylist always knows exactly what she has in her toolbox at all times, and knows what is available to work with. Pick out any stylish woman on the street and you can bet that she has an organized closet at home. And I guarantee that you will too, as soon as you begin to think of your clothes as tools. To begin, just follow these easy steps:

Separate your entire wardrobe into two seasons (warm and cold), and store away anything not suited to the current season. Sometimes it's difficult to put things away, but there really is no reason to battle a sea of sweaters to reach your strappy sundress when you really won't be wearing them for at least another three months. Also, be sure to store the unseasonable clothes in clean, dry storage bins or bags. Moths love old food stains and devour perspiration, and such bins will help your garments stay in good condition. Plus, you will have a better idea of what you want to keep as you unpack them in the correct season.

Now look at what is left. Pull out and put to the side all the garments that you don't currently wear, or haven't worn in the

19

Copyrighted Material

last six months. There will be various reasons and degrees of wear-ability. If you are on the fence about a garment, scan back through Chapter 2 and see if the item still seems passable, and remember that clothes that are worn out or don't fit are no good to you.

Replace all wire or plastic hangers with wooden ones. These will help your clothes retain their shape and condition.

Now group all your slacks together and hang; followed by skirts and then jackets. Notice how quickly your eyes put matches of tops and bottoms together, and how easily you can see all your tools.

Now add blouses and cotton blend shirts to hangers and hang. Place folded sweaters, knitwear and Lycra tops on the shelf, since putting them on hangers will cause the garments to stretch and lose their shape.

Finally, store dresses on hangers next to the blouses.

Now, place seasonal shoes at the bottom of your closet along with a box or bin that houses belts, scarves and other accessories. Bags can be stored on top if this bin or on the shelf if you have space.

Step back and take a look at your toolbox. This is your new working wardrobe. See how easy it is to create countless looks all because you can immediately see all that you have to work with? This is partly because the garments themselves have the power to inspire you. Hopefully, you also have your "Style Vision Board" hanging nearby for added inspiration.

Let's shift focus to the pile we created in Step #2. These are the clothes that you don't wear. As you begin to sort through, be honest about the clothes and the reasons you don't wear them. Say your reasons out loud. Hearing things like, "I will fit into it again, someday" or "I keep thinking I will find a use for it" will help you to let go of them.

Women are also known to keep a variety of sizes in their closets as well. Mainly due to normal fluctuations in weight, or yo-yo dieting, but I still find that it is just as important to store these

Copyrighted Material

items away with the seasonal ones so that you know everything in your closet fits you. Give away the rest.

If you have any clothes left that are well cut and fit you beautifully, or perhaps are expensive or have classic appeal, but don't fit in with your current style, save them as part of what we in the business call 'personal vintage.' These looks should be kept easily accessible so that you can bring them back out as designers revisit these styles. A great example is trouser pants. As the trend changes from flare leg to skinny leg and back again, you can recycle and revive your designer looks so that you don't have to repurchase them.

Normally, there would be nothing left in the "I never wear" pile, but if there is and you decide you want to keep these items, put them in the closet and re-review next season. The review session should be adhered to at least twice a year as you pack away or unpack your seasonal wardrobes. Or as you buy new clothes, you can make space for them by removing old or worn out items.

The last step to cleaning out your wardrobe is to decide on a mantra. Choose one that communicates the joy of feeling your best every day. Mine is: "Every day is like a Sunday and deserves my best." This reminds me that looking my best all the time is worth more than saving the effort for some fantasy day that may or may not come. Start today seeing your clothes as tools to support your journey to a more confident and radiant you.

Using Visual Subtleties to Your Advantage

I am sure that everyone has heard the old rules about watching out for horizontal stripes as they can make you look larger, or that wearing black will always make you look slimmer, but what most people don't realize is that all clothes, properly orchestrated, can create these illusions on their own. You see, all clothes create subtle lines, both horizontal and vertical. These lines can be produced with seams pleats, piping, yokes, waistbands, or hemlines. Now, because lines that run width-ways across your body create the illusion of width and shorten your body, you, as a standard sized gal, will want to look for lines that

21

Copyrighted Material

run the length of your body which will create the illusion of thinness and height. If you are more of a pear shape, you can even use subtle lines to help balance your body symmetry as learned in Chapter 2. For example, you could wear a flared A-line skirt that has vertical seams, pleats or print, which will lengthen the legs and narrow the hip area. Then pair it with a top that has subtle widening features at the chest area or neckline. This will visually narrow your bottom half, and subtly widen your top half to create an even body symmetry.

There are many different ways that you can use vertical lines to your advantage. Illusions running up and down the body will always elongate it, especially if the clothes are in the same color grouping or tone. For an extra lengthening effect, pair slacks with a closed toe shoe, and if you want to push it even farther, make sure the shoe matches tonally to the pant. This will make your legs appear to continue straight on to the tips of your toes. Conversely, wearing a contrasting colored shoe will shorten the leg. Another way to create length is to look for garments that have a vertical shape; ones that make vertical lines in themselves like, long-length garments, vertical seaming, stripes, zippers, fastenings, and garment layering (reveals panels of color through torso area). My favorite example that embodies almost all of these traits is a long, cable knit cardigan that I wear for both work and lounging around. The knit of the sweater creates vertical lines on its own, but the length also creates a visual line that runs down to my legs. All that coupled with a solid undershirt that creates a color panel down my middle, framed by the buttons down one side and the button holes down the other. So, that's three more vertical lines I added by not buttoning the cardigan!

Horizontal lines can be a little bit trickier to use because most women don't want any part of their body appear larger or wider. I can assure you, however, that a properly placed horizontal line can give a body balance. They can also create a visual punctuation on a tall body, but should be used sparingly on someone who is shorter.

Horizontal lines can be formed with seams, prints,

22

Copyrighted Material

yokes, paneling, ribbing, shirring, fabric bands, by creating a color break, wearing a belt, and garment layering to produce horizontal slabs of color. Remember that a horizontal line is something you only want a small amount of. You will not want to look for outfits that have more than two of the above features. Also, remember that placement of these features is key. A horizontal line will draw the eyes' focus, to that area as well. If you are unsure where the focus lies in a garment, simply look at it head on, and cover one eye. Whatever area your eye is drawn to is the focus of that garment.

Using color to your advantage will be one of the best assets in your style arsenal, and there is so much that can be said about color too. I will try to keep it as simple as possible here. Like lines, color has the ability to draw the eye to wherever it is placed. You can use it to play up or down certain parts of your body, but keeping in mind that dark colors minimize the area they cover, while bright or light colors will highlight the areas they cover.

When using color to look your best, start with ones that flatter your skin tone. I mean, you can wear whatever color you want, but the shade of color should be tonally consistent with your skin. We will use blue as an example as there are many different shades of blue, from robin's egg blue to midnight blue. If you are pale, choose a shade that is not pigment intense like baby blue. If you have medium skin tone, then a medium amount of pigment is best, like cornflower blue. If you're darker, you can go all the way, but be careful of very light shades as they can make you look washed out.

If you are unsure what colors work best for you, there is a test. Take the garment of questionable color and a mirror outside, as daylight is always preferable to electric light. Then hold the garment up to your chin and look at it in the mirror. The sunlight will reflect the color up under your chin, your nose and your eyebrows. Does the color add a wonderful glow to your skin or does it look terrible and you don't know why? I for example like to stay away from yellow and green because I have a very

23

Copyrighted Material

yellow skin tone and it makes me look sickly. I play this down by wearing a lot of blue or bluish pink. You should try this with some of the clothes that you already have, but be prepared to look at some pieces in a whole new light.

The last visual subtlety you can use to your advantage is print. Like color, prints or patterns can be used to draw the eye to the area it covers. There are three crucial aspects of proper print use: all over print, weight of print and placement of print.

First, let's talk about placement of print. This means that you have to pay careful attention to where the print is on your body, because print, no matter the size, creates focus and interest to where it is placed. For example, if you want to disguise the lower half of your body, then dress it in a dark solid color, and then use print to draw focus to the top half of your body. This trick also works in reverse.

Another crucial aspect of print is weight, or the size of the print. A large sized print will create the appearance of smallness, where a small print can serve to add volume. Again, think about this visual print when considering your placement of print. You may not want to wear a small print skirt if you are trying to hide wide hips or thicker thighs.

Last of the crucial aspects of print is all over print. This of course, is seen mainly with dresses, and can be used to created visual harmony between all parts of the body. This is especially effective when paired with neutral accessories and outer garments. Remember to incorporate what you just learned about weight of print. Being average size, you may not want to wear a small weighted print all over your body as it could make you look larger.

There are many different ways you can use these subtleties to produce visual illusions, which you can use to disguise your weaknesses and highlight your strengths, here are a few more tips to keep in mind when dressing and shopping:

Look for tops or dresses that have a seam that changes direction. For example, a seam that runs horizontally from the sides across

Copyrighted Material

the chest and then goes vertically down under the breasts creating a "Y" shape. This shrinks the waistline while adding fullness to the bosom. Another way to accomplish this by zipping up a coat or buttoning up a cardigan to just below the bust.

As an average sized woman, you may choose to stick with in one color grouping as it will add to your height. Remember to stick with a tone that suits your skin, and then create an outfit from similar tones, like pink and lilac or cream and beige. Match your shoes and bag to continue the lengthening effect.

Wear prints that are medium to large sized, and avoid smaller prints as they will make you appear strangely large.

Color placement, like print placement, can also be used to your advantage. Use color and/or print to draw the eye to the part of your body that you want people to zero in on. Put focus on the top one-third of your body to produce height, or put it on the bottom to shorten you. Unless you are verging on top heavy, the most flattering look for you will be a light or bright top coupled with a dark bottom.

If you like a particular color, but it doesn't suit your skin tone, wear it on the lower half of your body. That way it is far enough away not to be able to reflect light onto your face.

Use horizontal effect print across an area that you want to form width and vertical effect print up and down the body to give the illusion of narrowing and elongation.

Wear a panel of color up and down the middle portion of your body to create another narrowing effect.

Closet Exercise #3: Know What You're Shopping For

Now that you have figured out your style signature, and we have accomplished the closet cleanout, there is just one more project for you to finish. This is more of a long-term project, however, and it's not something you can complete immediately as you will have to shift your mental state when shopping and that can take a few practice runs to get the hang of it.

Copyrighted Material

Think about your newly organized closet, everything is in order and you know where everything is. It may even be looking a little bare if you had too many items that didn't flatter your figure, and that means shopping! But before you run out with your credit card, you need to start thinking and shopping like a stylist. You will also need to think about clothes in four basic categories, and if you master this, you will automatically know what items go together and when changes need made.

Group One is the "High Fashion" or "Trendy" clothes, and will be filled with clothes that are in and out of the shops seasonally. Mostly, they are directly influenced by the catwalks and change frequently. They can also be bold, loud, or even extreme, but these clothes are great for experimenting. I would only spend a small amount of money on clothes in this group because the speed of fashion is so fast. You will need to wear these looks to death before they are considered "out." This is good though, because you will tire of them that way. They will be just as sick of you too, so I would donate them at the end of the season.

What to look for: Statement tops, playful accessories, dresses, colorful shoes, or the latest wrap. It's important to note that a lot of times, seasonal trends tend to flatter a specific body type. If this applies to you one season or another, buy up the more classic garments within the look because they won't be there next season.

Group Two is the "Clothes" group, which may sound ordinary, but these are your fun pieces that last a few seasons. Every woman has her favorite outfit or style that flatters her body, and those pieces fall into this group as well. You should spend a little more on these items as you will want to get more use out of them. Keep a look out for high quality, like good fabrics, linings and trimmings.

What to look for: denim skirts with flattering shapes, and a classic feel, jeans, lightweight jackets, fitted shirts and shapely sweaters.

Copyrighted Material

Group Three is all about the "Classics." These are the garments every woman must have in her closet. For example, "the little black dress," "the classic trouser pant" or "the impeccably fitted suit," which can all be dressed up with the latest trend accessories. Clothes in this group will be classic styles that don't age, so spend what you can afford on these items, but look for sales to get the best value for your dollar. Also, get used to planning shopping trips ahead of time to take advantage of upcoming sales. A list may even be helpful as this will keep you from buying items that you do not need just because they are drastically reduced.

Don't forget that for these timeless looks, fit is everything. If your shape is not well enough catered to in mainstream stores, then look up a good dressmaker or tailor to make up the pieces you plan to keep for a long time. It's not as expensive as you might think, if you compare the cost against years of confidence, joy and the knowledge that you can always rely on these garments to give you an air of sophisticated grooming. Trousers and jackets are crucial for fit, so they would be a great place to start. Plus, once the dressmaker has your measurements, you can wait for fabric sales and save it for when you are ready for the garment to be made.

What to look for: the perfect (classic cut/excellent fit) black trouser, a classic jacket and skirt combo, a suit, and a timeless coat such as the classic trench or pea coat. Also, look for cashmere knitwear, a sleek pair of leather boots and a beautiful leather handbag that holds its shape.

Group Four is just the "Basics." This is your T-shirts, yoga or sweatpants, knitwear, fleece, etc. The items in this group need not be trend oriented, unless you want them to be. When shopping for basics save time and money by shopping in catalogues or online since fit will be less of an issue.

Just remember, when you buy new garments, clear out anything old so that your wardrobe doesn't slowly expand to overfull. Donate your gently used clothes to thrift stores or even

Copyrighted Material

your friends, so that someone else can get some enjoyment from your clothes too. The only reason to keep something is if it is timeless in design and will age beautifully, like a leather handbag. Main street fashion certainly doesn't age well as they just aren't meant to last.

Once you have taken a few shopping trips and followed these guidelines you will have many "basics" and "classics" to mix with your "high fashion" items or other "clothes." You should try to update each group seasonally and inexpensively. And if you're ever in doubt, remember that it's better to have a few impeccably fitted clothes that showcase you in your best light, than it is to have lots of badly fitted garments that just fill up your closet.

Finishing Touches

Thus far, I have given you many things to consider when choosing what to wear. You know what works for your body, and hopefully we have boosted your self esteem a few notches. But now it's time to talk about accessory choices. Like clothes, accessory styles are driven by season. One season you will see tiny clutches lining the store shelves and the next thing you know, its slouchy hobo bags. Just think about sunglass styles morphing from Jon Lennon style wire frames to the big Jackie-O style widescreens. But what may be fashionable may not be what is best for you. Accessories are the sprinkles to your cupcake; they give your final look its polish. When you find one or two statement pieces that draw focus to where they are placed, you ooze confidence and sophistication. When you finish dressing each day, stand back and look at what you have created and then carefully and critically add any accessories that will produce more balance.

Once you understand how to balance your body you will always make effortless choices, and accessorizing will be a breeze. Here are some things to consider when making these accessory choices:

Your bra. Usually considered a part of underwear rather than an

28

Copyrighted Material

accessory, I am placing it here because it is as important as putting your shoes on before leaving the house. A correctly fitted bra can make an entire outfit by accentuating your waist, because your bust sits higher on your ribcage. Ensure your straps are properly adjusted every day. I can recall countless times where I only needed to adjust a bra to produce a smoother silhouette. The correct cup size and bandwidth will also give you the comfort you deserve and brightens another important accessory-your smile.

When choosing a handbag, look for sizes and shapes that are proportionate to your body. Average to large ladies should always go with a medium to large sized bag that has structure and holds its shape. This is actually quite simple to follow everyday and you can notice a difference immediately. For example, I always advise pregnant women to carry an oversized bag, that way it competes with the stomach for focus.

Remember to balance things like bags, jewelry, belts, and eyewear together by making sure they are of similar weight and size. For instance, large statement jewelry pieces should be coupled with a large bag or large sunglasses. Standard sized women should avoid tiny accessories as a general rule. Skinny belts, small bags, thin necklaces, tiny stud earrings, or small rings will make you look oddly larger.

Color is still a factor when picking the right sunglasses. Apply the pigment rule we discussed in the last chapter. You will want to match the tone of the frame or colored lens to your skin and hair tone. For example, if you have dark hair and dark skin, you can go for bolder tones, but blondes or fair skinned ladies should look for rose or amber colored glasses. The size rule applies here too; a small pair of frames will make your face appear larger.

 Keep color in mind when deciding on accessories, if you choose a bright and noticeable color, the eye will inevitably be drawn there. So, if you fall in love with a neon green hipster belt, you will be drawing attention to your hips.

Choose shoes that have a chunky heel or wedge. This will create the illusion of shapely calves and dainty ankles. If your feet are

29

Copyrighted Material

more on the wide side, a pointed-toe shoe creates the feeling of narrowness. Think about thin strappy shoes with thin soles or skinny heels, because you may need something more substantial to create balance. Also, steer clear of ankle straps that foreshorten the leg.

Now that you have chosen your outfit, and properly accessorized it you can admire all the hard work. And it is work, but only in the beginning. Soon, you will be choosing your clothes and accessories confidently and easily. But, I want to empower you immediately! So, I have arranged a few key questions to ask yourself each day as you assess your clothing choices. These questions will help you practice what you have learned in this book as you make your way to being a stylish and confident woman.

Does your silhouette have a fitted or shapeless outline?

Do your color choices reflect positively or negatively to your skin tone?

Are the colors you chose to wear from the same color grouping or from opposite ends of the spectrum?

Do your fabric choices show a flat personality or are they stiff and lifeless? Or do they portray ease of movement and feminine softness?

Are any of your garments unwittingly drawing focus to the widest part of your body?

Are your accessories providing the balance your body and shape need?

These questions are crucial to keep in mind. Apply them daily and soon you will find that you won't even need to question your choices in the future. Style and sophistication will become habit.

Create a Stunning Wardrobe on Purpose

If you haven't guessed it already, the trick to dressing for your body shape is all about where you draw the eye. Understanding how to use details such as jewelry, color, pattern, and print can

Copyrighted Material

give you that poise and self assurance that others just can't quite put their finger on. In this book I have given you all my secrets on how to accomplish the perfect look for your particular body shape.

I hope that you will embody your new image and embrace the style you have chosen. Don't get discouraged or be too hard on yourself if you can't immediately remodel your entire wardrobe. Changing your image takes time, and money. Let's face it; in this turbulent economy buying new clothes is low on the priority list. But recognizing that every clothing purchase you make from now on will be chosen affordably and on purpose is a step in the right direction.

The most important thing to keep in mind while shopping is to only look for the items you need and avoid buying garments that do not fill a gap in your wardrobe. Because we invest such emotion into our clothes and expect them to make us feel thinner, shapelier or taller, we feel like we have failed when the resulting purchase doesn't give us the comfort high we expected. But if you can remove the feelings attached to shopping and assess your body objectively and apply what you have learned here, you can make big changes to your look. Turn your thinking around to take a less emotional view, I promise it will be more effective.

I have been following this philosophy myself for many years by dressing in colors that compliment my skin tone, garments that suit my body shape and accessories that highlight my best features. But I don't love every piece; I just know they work for me. It helps me, especially before shopping, to think about my "outfits" as uniforms. I mean we all wear uniforms to some extent, and I have quite a few that have served me well. Taking an unemotional approach to my clothes has not only helped me determine what I need, but it also narrows my potential for time wasting. Below are some examples of uniforms I wear.

The "At Work" or "Authoritative" Uniform: These are my mostly grey and black clothes, because office days are usually long, and any number of accidents can happen during lunch meetings and

Copyrighted Material

styling appointments behind the scenes of TV or magazines. Tailored suits and hair put back not only look chic, but they portray the air of authority for me in the work place. This is especially crucial if I need to look somewhat stern, or if I am pitching to a new client. Messy hair and unkempt clothing do not say "efficient."

The "Work at Home" or "Writing at the Office" Uniform: This is my jeans or fitted khakis paired with comfortable boots or ballet flats. I prefer to wear tops that cover my middle so I don't feel obligated to hold it in. I will also choose pants that have a little Lycra in them to stretch and accommodate sitting for long periods of time. Any restrictive fabrics can be terribly uncomfortable to work in.

The "Workshop" or "Stage" Uniform: You might think that this uniform would be the same as the "Authoritative" uniform, but it is not. I have tried to conduct my workshops in black, but the make me appear too grim and unyielding on stage. The bright lights used require vivid colors and bold shapes. I will often buy pieces for these uniforms that I wouldn't normally wear anywhere else because they would be too attention seeking. Shoes are also really important here. I try to remember that the audience is nearly eye level with my feet so I may wear "showy" heels that look great. Often times, flashy shoes are not very comfortable and can only be worn for a short period of time, but that works great with this uniform because nothing in this group is meant to be worn for more than a few hours.

The "Weekend" Uniform: My friends and colleagues are the ones I dress for, and I mainly wear this uniform when I am meeting them for dinner, or catching a movie. I put more effort into these uniforms than I do the others because my friends inspire me and we share ideas. Even though amongst these women are designers, TV presenters, writers and magazine publishers, doesn't mean it's all about the labels either. It's about individuality; it's all about looking and feeling good, isn't it? I love mixing and matching designer pieces with others that I picked up in a second-hand store.

Copyrighted Material

The "Visiting the 'Rents" or "Country" Uniform: I like to get out of the city and unwind as often as I can. It's about as far from high fashion as you can get, and if I drive straight in from the city, I can feel very out of place. Bright colors and funky designs have no place there and can attract a lot of attention. Besides, pointy heels and boots sink deeply into mud.

The "Special Occasion" Uniform: This uniform is pretty self-explanatory. These are the clothes that have that out of the ordinary "evening" feeling. Personally, I prefer designs that are monochrome. My favorite "go to" evening look is a tightly fitted waistcoat with cleavage and skillfully cut trousers a la Yves St. Laurent. This classic look can come across as a little dull so I always make sure to indulge in a fantastic pair of designer shoes that polish the whole look.

Thinking about your clothes as uniforms is a handy way to quickly assess your wardrobe needs before going shopping or browsing online. This will also help you focus on the coming tasks, and knowing that you will be properly dressed for them means you will no longer have to think about what you are wearing. Don't browse or surf without cause, and only visit stores when you have located a gap in your wardrobe or you have worn out a key piece and need to replace it.

If you have found a reason to take a shopping trip, or your favorite designer is having a sale, try to remember these final tips that will help you create your stunning wardrobe on purpose.

Start with a budget and stick to it.

Only visit the stores that you know have a good fit for you.

Wear clothes that are easily removable. You will discourage yourself from trying a garment on if the one you are currently wearing is too difficult to get on and off.

Take wipes. We all get hot and bothered when trying on many clothes, especially in the summer months or bathing suit shopping.

Never buy anything intending to lose weight to fit into it.

33

Copyrighted Material

Some clothes can be appealing on the hanger like flouncy feminine blouses, but they disappoint in the dressing room. Instead, study the item carefully and assess the features. Know whether it will suit your body shape before trying it on.

Use a store's sizing as a guide only. There is no need to get hung up by a number on a tag. It's all about the fit, so if your normal size 14 is too tight in the bust, but the 16 fits like a dream and lies beautifully, buy the 16. If the thought of a larger size is that much of an issue, cut the label out when you get home.

Whenever you find yourself ready to purchase an item, visually match it with other pieces of your wardrobe. What will you wear it with? Where will you where it? If you can't visualize either of these things, then don't buy it.

Set yourself a time limit. This will minimize impulse buying. If you haven't found what you're looking for when time is up, ask the sales representative when the next shipment arrives and reschedule to come back then.

Catalog of Fashion Choices "The Guide"

Welcome to the Guide section of the "How to Dress for Your Body Shape". Here I have catalogued some common items you will find in stores or online. I cover everything from appropriate neckline or hemline for your shape to the right shoe or handbag to balance your look.

To be user friendly, each illustration has been marked with a symbol that tells you whether or not it will work for your particular body shape.

✔ When you see this symbol, know that this particular style is just right for you.

Copyrighted Material

X Avoid any styles that have this symbol as they are not flattering to your body shape.

? Any clothing style associated with this symbol are the ones that may or may not work for you. Decide yourself based on all the other criteria you have learned about in this book.

Necklines

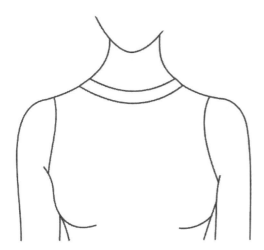

Crew/Round Neck X This is a fitted neckline, which hugs the base of the neck. It is usually found on knitwear. A high neckline like this will always make a neck look shorter.

Copyrighted Material

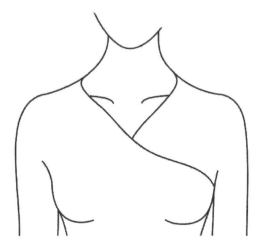

Ballerina Neck **?** This is a high wrap that generally has less depth   than an ordinary v-neckline. You will find it in knitwear or tops.

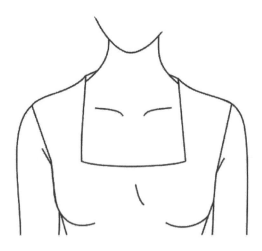

Copyrighted Material

Square Neck ✔ This can be found in tops, dresses and occasionally in knitwear.

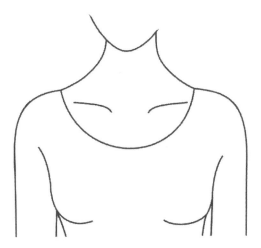

Scoop Neck ✔ This is a low round shaped neckline that looks like a semi-circle. It is flattering to all shapes and will give an elegant neckline and more attention to the bust line whether or not there is cleavage.

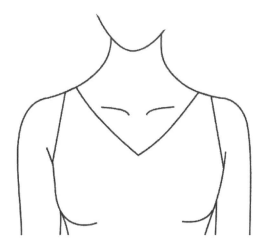

V Neck ✔ This is an elegant neckline with a v- shaped drop. A high v-neck is often found in knitwear and a lower v-neck is found in Lycra tops, wrap tops or wrap dresses.

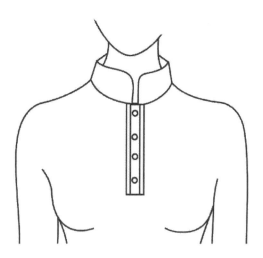

Copyrighted Material

Mandarin Neck ✗ This is a high collar that dips at the center and is always found on a garment that fastens through the middle. It has a very high buttoned-up, almost strict feel.

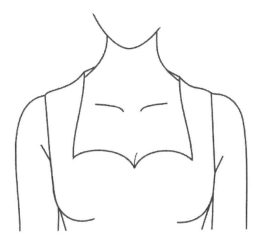

Sweetheart Neck ✔ This is usually found in clothing that has no 'give' fabrics because the design must hold its shape. The shoulder will drop vertically then a dainty curved line runs over each breast.

Copyrighted Material

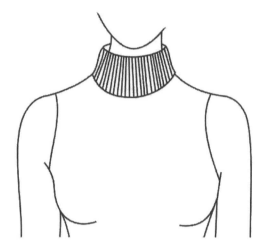

Turtle Neck ✗ This is nearly always found in knitwear as a fine gauge piece of knitting.

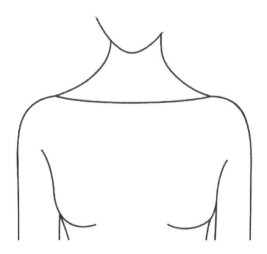

Boat Neck ✗ This is a neckline that appears to go straight

Copyrighted Material

across the body from shoulder to shoulder. It will widen the shoulder area and in some cases can shorten the appearance of the neck.

Collared Neck **X** There is a huge variety of collars to choose from, the most common being the straight collar that encloses the neck when it is done up.

Copyrighted Material

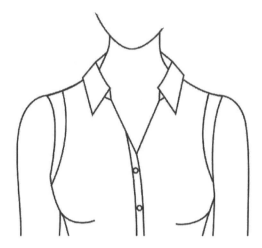

Open-Collared Neck ✔ This differs from above as it is worn undone to create a soft and blurred v-neckline. There isn't a woman alive who will not look good in a fitted shirt, which is sexily undone.

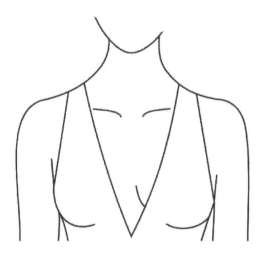

Copyrighted Material

Plunge Neckline ✔ This neckline will have varying degrees of plunge. It requires an excellent bra but can also be carried off by wearing another layer underneath.

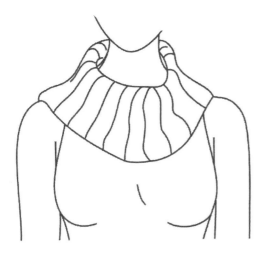

Large Polo Neck ✔ This neckline always appears on a chunky piece of knitwear and can stand up fairly stiff around the neck in a wide circle.

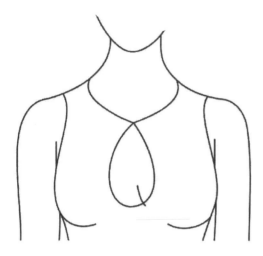

Tear Drop Neck **?** This style is effectively like a high boat neck but has an extra teardrop shape cut out that may or may not show cleavage.

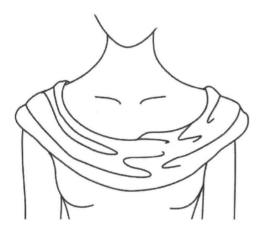

Cowl Neck **X** This is scoop neckline with an extra layer of

Copyrighted Material

fabric that hangs loosely over the bust to add volume. It will bulk up the bust area and draw the eye to it.

Showing Shoulders

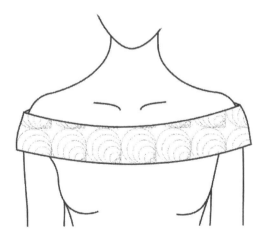

Bardot Style ✗ This top has the widest of all necklines and was popularized by the actress Brigitte Bardot. This band will widen your shoulders and give your body a feeling of foreshortening.

45

Copyrighted Material

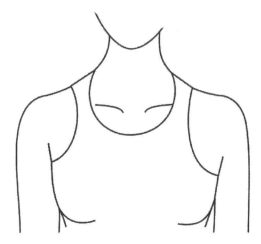

Low Wrap Style (No Sleeves) ✔ This shape with wide neckline and sleeves placed wide on the shoulders widens the area around the neckline and bust and reduces the amount of shoulder on show.

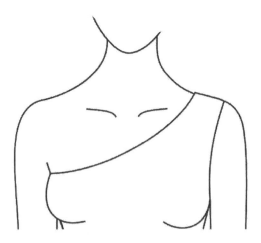

Copyrighted Material

Asymmetric Shoulder ✔ This comes in and out of fashion and suits all shoulder shapes. It is a dramatic and chic statement for gowns and tops alike.

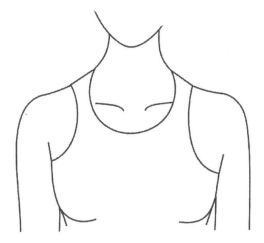

High Neck Vest ✗ The neck area is made smaller and the shoulder area is increased because the straps are pushed further towards the neck.

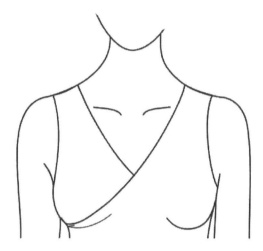

Wide Strap Vest ✔ The neck area is widened with this design and the wide straps cover a larger area of shoulder making it a good look for larger bodies in general.

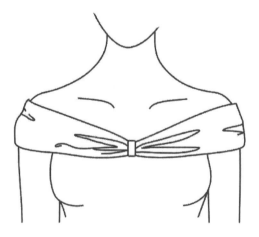

Copyrighted Material

Off The Shoulder ✔ This neckline works very well because of the gentle v-shape creates a flattering effect for curvy upper bodies and standard shapes.

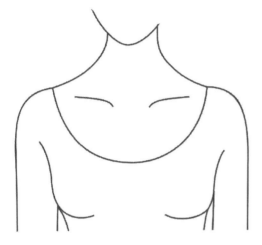

Wide Scoop ✔ This neckline can work very well to create a subtle width across the shoulder area.

Copyrighted Material

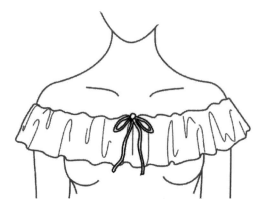

Gypsy Style ✔ This is a great garment for feminizing the shoulders and for this reason is the best choice if you are broad shouldered but like the idea of wearing styles that have an obvious horizontal feature.

Copyrighted Material

Open Backs

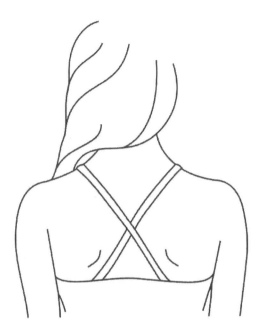

Crossover **?** Often appears on special occasion dresses. The effect of these thin straps criss-crossing across the back is to make shoulders appear larger and therefore the waist smaller.

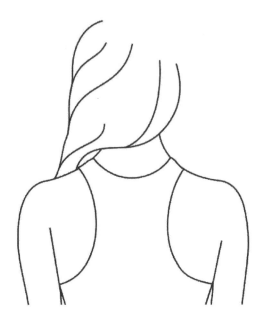

T-Bar (Sports Top) **?** The straps are designed to make the shoulders appears larger and more sporty. But it can draw attention to shoulders and to make the upper torso seem more developed.

Copyrighted Material

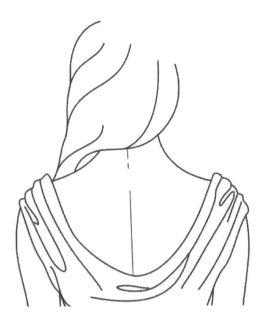

Cowl Back **?** The straps are placed wide apart and a gentle draping cowl feminizes and softens the back, but depending on the design can also make your back appear wider.

Copyrighted Material

Strapless Styles

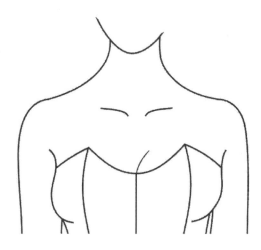

Period Style ✔ This design has a gothic feel to it and often appears as cocktail gowns or corset tops. This shape will minimize the bust area.

Copyrighted Material

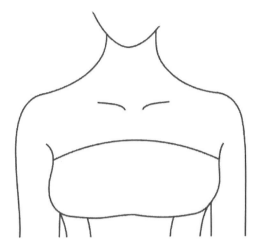

Curved ✗ A design like this creates a larger area at the bust, and because it does not follow a horizontal line to mirror the shoulder line it will exaggerate square shoulders.

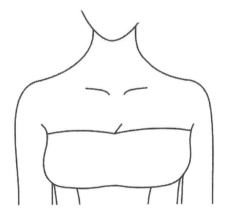

Copyrighted Material

Large Band Across the Bust **?** This design adds volume at the bust as well as width, making the waist look smaller by comparison. Many bodices will have embellishments here which also create volume.

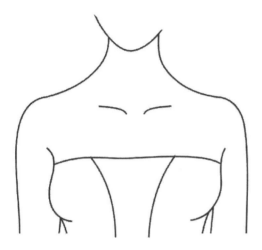

Standard Strapless **?** This is a universally flattering shape with vertical seaming through the front of the body. The vertical seeming will always make the waist appear more streamlined.

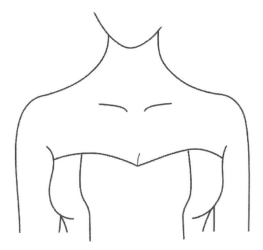

Scalloped ✔ This design suggests softness and femininity. The scallop over the bust will create a minimizing effect and will also soften the shoulders.

Sleeve Styles

Copyrighted Material

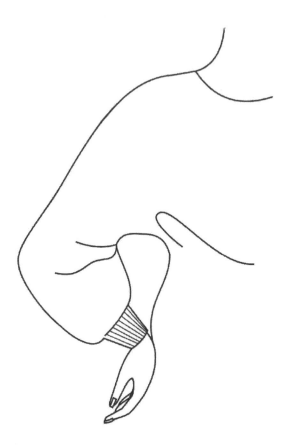

Batwing Sleeves **?** This style usually appears in soft jersey fabrics or fine knitwear and is an interesting and forgiving shape. It will disguise the shape of any arm but can foreshorten a body.

Copyrighted Material

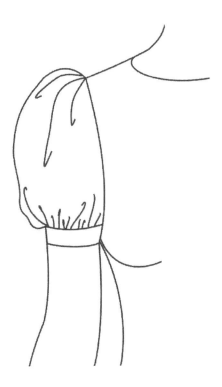

Puffed Sleeve **?** This is a great device for creating width and volume around the shoulder area. It works well for curvy arms by appearing larger in size than the piece of arm on show and therefore balancing the arm.

Copyrighted Material

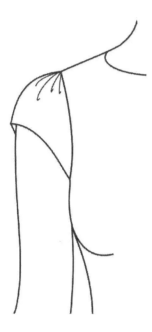

Capped Sleeves **X** This design concentrates on the shoulder and top area of the arm. It can accentuate the size of this area and is a popular choice for those who enjoy the way their arm looks more athletic and toned.

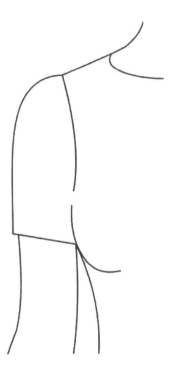

Fitted Sleeve **?** A hard horizontal line across the arm where it begins to widen is a way of looking muscular. The t-shirt was invented after all by the US Army as an undergarment.

Copyrighted Material

Angel Sleeve ✔ This is a great sleeve for fuller softer arms. It will always work to make the arm look smaller and more feminine.

Copyrighted Material

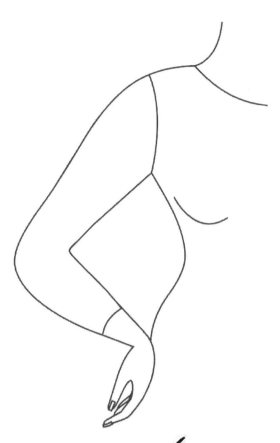

Three Quarter Length ✔ This length sleeve works perfectly to make limbs look longer and, when designed with a wide flare, will be one of the most flattering shapes for curvy arms and wrists.

Copyrighted Material

Bell Bottom Sleeve ✔ A long and wide sleeve will work to balance the top of the arm. As a general rule a curvier arm needs a wider flare at the bottom.

Copyrighted Material

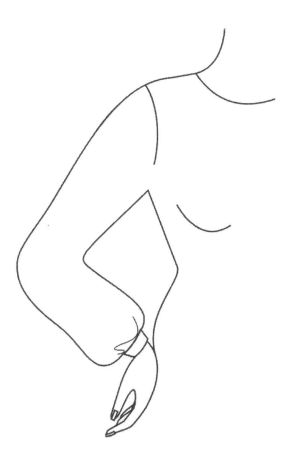

Bell Capped Sleeve ✔ A sleeve like this will come in and out of fashion and is most often seen on formal or special occasion wear blouses. It works well to widen the bottom part of the arm and will give balance to the top part.

Copyrighted Material

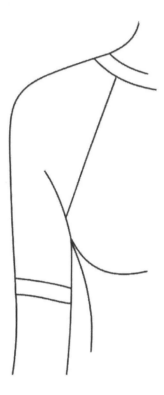

Raglan Sleeve **?**   This design is more to do with the way that the sleeve fits into the shoulder area because it is not a conventional sleeve casing. It is often used in sport clothing because it allows for more give across the back. It also enlarges the shoulder area especially if it appears where the sleeve is a contrasting color from the body.

Open Slash Sleeve ✔ This sleeve is sometimes slashed from the shoulder to the wrist, but some designs have a slash just at the top of the arm or several slashes that are caught at various points along the way. This is a perfect sleeve for concealing the shape of the arm, and creating a vertical line.

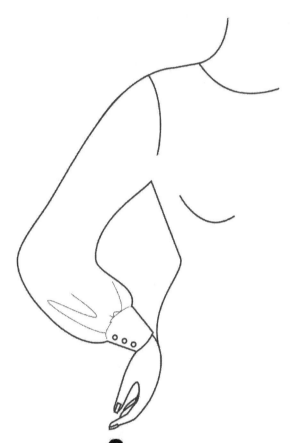

Extended Cuff **?** A dressy shirt, blouse or top can use this feature and it is a great one to reduce the appearance of a long slender arm, especially if there is some gathering into the cuff that creates width around the forearm.

Top Styles

Copyrighted Material

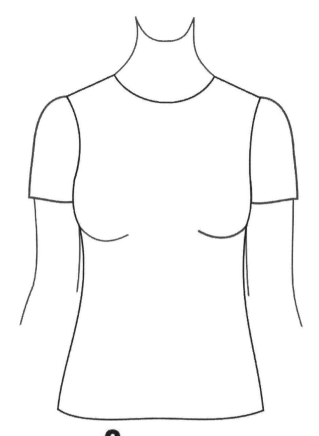

Classic T-Shirt **?** This shape usually has a little Lycra to help it stretch or it is a loose weave cotton so we can stretch it over our heads. It has become a utility garment of modern day times and is useful for casual wear.

Copyrighted Material

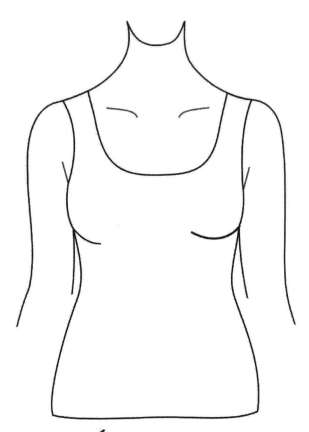

Classic Vest ✔ The vest has just that bit more shape to it and so is a more flattering garment for summer. It is also a very useful garment to wear under another for a layered look.

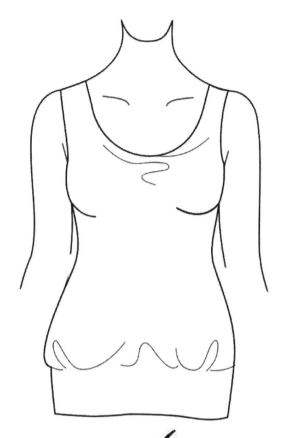

Blousy-Dropped Waist ✔ This top can have any type of neckline. The best feature is the soft gathered fabric around the tummy area and the low-waisted band that gently masks the shape of your whole upper torso.

Copyrighted Material

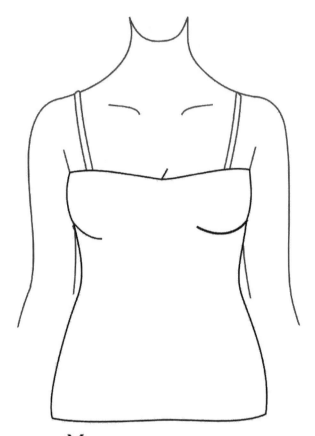

Camisole **X** This is a top that normally appears in flimsy fabrics. It gives little or no shape to curves but is good for slender frames. Worn either braless or with a good strapless bra it can look very demure and looks great with jeans.

Copyrighted Material

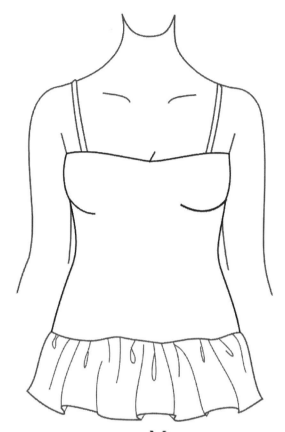

Camisole with Peplum **X** All of the above counts here but the important thing about this top is its extended length. Any top with a peplum or loose layer like this can add volume to the lower tummy and hips.

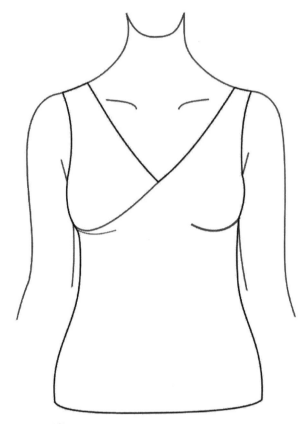

Wrap ✔ This is a flattering shape that wraps the body and creates definition at the waist.

Fitted Shirt ✔ This is a classic that is adapted to suit every body shape and is flattering to both curvy and slender alike. Petite retailers will always offer shorter lengths for instance and tall retailers will add extra length.

Copyrighted Material

Smock Top ✗ This is a top with a lot of fabric in it. In general it will widen the shoulders, blur any definition between bust and tummy and add volume to the whole upper torso.

Copyrighted Material

Empire Line ✔ This is very flattering and easy to wear. The difference between empire and smock is that the fabric is fitted over the bust and pulled close to the body creating definition and then disguising the tummy.

Copyrighted Material

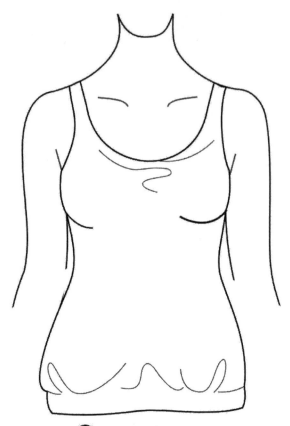

Drop Waist ❓ Tops that have a dropped waist are a joy to wear because the waist and tummy is not on show; however, the dropped waist draws the eye line downwards, creating some foreshortening.

Copyrighted Material

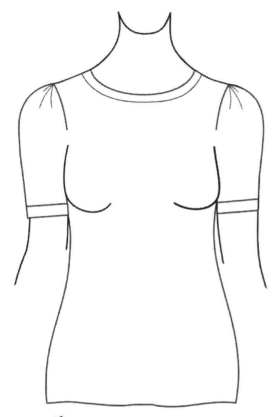

Tunic ✔ This is one of the most popular shapes of recent times, creating a loose layer over the whole of the upper body and covering waistline and tummy.

Jackets

Copyrighted Material

Fitted Streamlined ✔ This jacket comes in a variety of styles but is identified by its lack of features and undefined waist. It is a classic style and often in a soft leather.

Copyrighted Material

Single Breasted **?** This is a universally flattering jacket. Often, it is fastened by only one or two buttons and has a fitted waist and small pockets at the hips. Remember, the fit is the most important feature.

Fitted/Detailed **?** This is a much more sporting shape with features like collar and cuff detail. It will usually appear in denim and corduroy. But beware; the extra pockets will add volume to the upper body.

Copyrighted Material

Double Breasted **?** This style has a sporting feel and appears when women's suiting takes on a more androgynous feel. Buttons may also be exaggerated in size and lapels large.

Copyrighted Material

Trench ✔ The jacket may fasten with subtle buttons or it may just wrap over. The crucial feature is the belted waist. This is a great way to define the upper body and is universally flattering.

Copyrighted Material

Cropped **X** This jacket is designed to change the proportions of a body making the lower body look streamlined. This style will create volume around the upper body.

Dresses

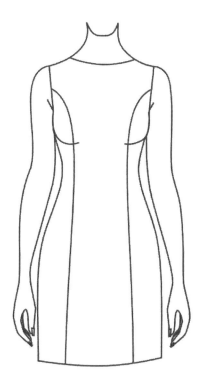

Shift Dress ✗ This is a short dress that has a sixties feel to it. It is often in stiffer fabrics like starched or treated cotton so it does not mould to the body. Not a particularly flattering shape, however.

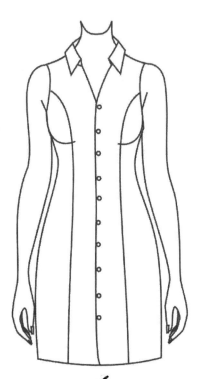

Shirt Dress ✔ A lovely classic style of dress with a central fastening through the middle of the body which creates a vertical line and will elongate the body. This is universally flattering style because it is gently fitted to the body.

Copyrighted Material

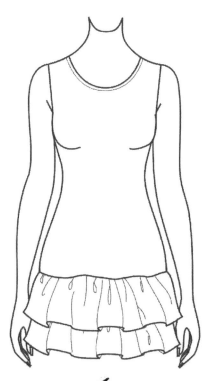

Drop Waist ✔ Changing the proportions of the waist, as this dress does, will always create a longer leaner line through the centre of the body. But placing the waist so much lower down the body takes the eyes downwards.

Wrap ✔ This has become a classic style, made in a figure hugging fabric like jersey; it is very flattering for most body shapes because of the definition it goes to the upper torso.

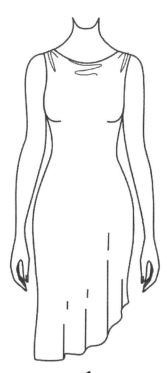

Bias Cut ✔ Any dress that is cut on the bias has stretch within the fabric and will wrap around the hips gently. It appears as a day dress as well as for evening and is a very sensual style.

Copyrighted Material

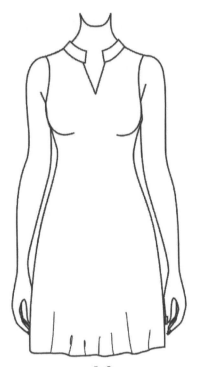

Tunic Dress **X** Like the shift dress, this style is pretty unforgiving and does not mold itself to the body's form. It is always pared down and has a strict slightly androgynous look making it good for formal and working situations.

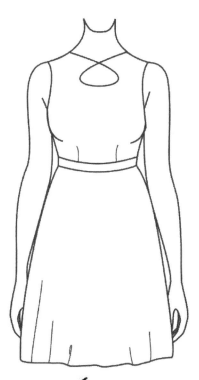

Waisted ✔ A classic style of dress that is fitted to the upper body and then flares out from the waist. This style draws the eye straight to the waist.

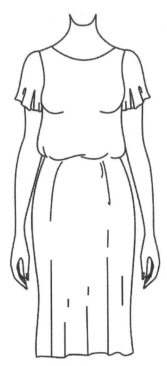

Blouson **X** This is a loose fitting dress that may be strapless as shown here or it may have sleeves. The elasticized waist blouses out around the upper torso adding volume to the top part of the body.

Copyrighted Material

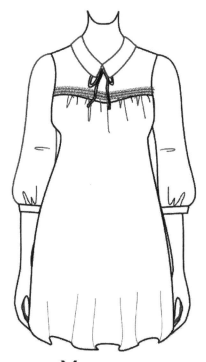

Smock **X** This has a fitted yoke that eases into a gathered effect across the cleavage. It will always add volume to this area.

Skirts

Copyrighted Material

Flared ✔ Some styles can be noticeably flared and some more subtle, bordering on an A-line style skirt. This will be your most versatile choice of skirt simply because it hides any hip or bottom shape and focuses on the waist.

Copyrighted Material

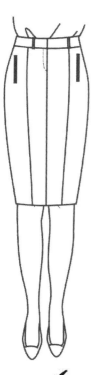

Pencil ✔ This classic style elongates legs because it is tapered at the back, like a small vent to allow you to take large enough steps to walk. It will work best with a heel to give the feet a tapered look.

Yoke and Flare ✔ This style of skirt is fitted to the hips and then flared from the hips It has the appearance of lowering the waist.

Copyrighted Material

Handkerchief Hemline ✔ This skirt will always look edgy or quirky because of the uneven effect around the hemline. For it to work well the focus must be on the legs, and therefore takes the eye line to the lower half of the body.

Circle ✔ This is a shape that is dictated by fashion and will appear from time to time. The interpretation of the volume of the circle will be up to you.

Bias ✔ This style of skirt looks sensual and feminine and, because it is cut on the bias of the fabric, will have plenty of give.

Copyrighted Material

Tiered ✔ A tiered skirt has a gypsy feel to it and is often seen as a versatile summer or casual wear look. Be careful though, because of the horizontal lines it has a widening effect.

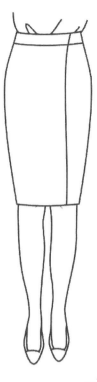

Wrap Front ✔ This style of skirt has a classic appeal and can appear as a tailored skirt or pared for a more casual look. It is usually fitted to the body around the waist and hips and has a straight silhouette from the hips to the knees. Because of the vertical line through the body it will always make the legs appear longer.

Copyrighted Material

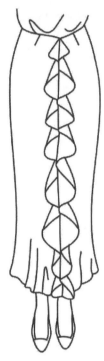

Vertical Ruffle ✔ This style of skirt has the same feminine appeal as the tiered skirt but a much longer line and therefore creates a more streamlining and lengthening effect.

Trousers and Pants

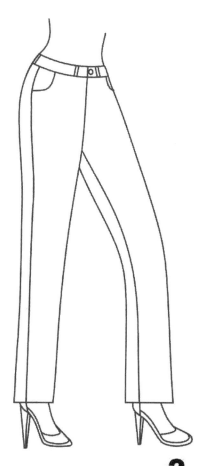

Fly Front/Straight Leg **?** This style of trouser is copied from
the Italian cut of men's trouser and is masculine in feel with a
straight leg. It will often have a lower waistband too just like the
men's version.

Copyrighted Material

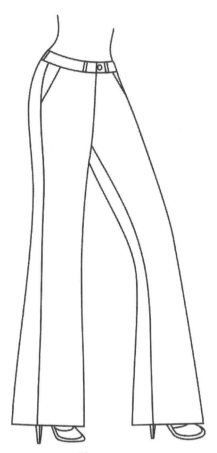

Flared ✔ This design of trouser is the most flattering for a woman's body because the wide flared hem line will always balance curvy thighs and add volume to slender ones. Make sure you spend time getting the fit right and this style will disguise the shape of legs and thighs with excellent results.

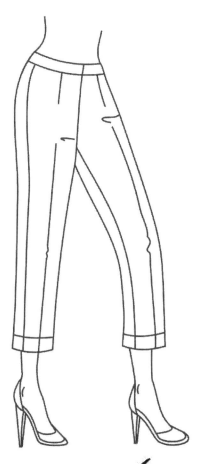

Cropped Trousers ✔ This is a very flattering cut with a classy choice of footwear. The hemline should be level with the lower calf, not the widest part.

Copyrighted Material

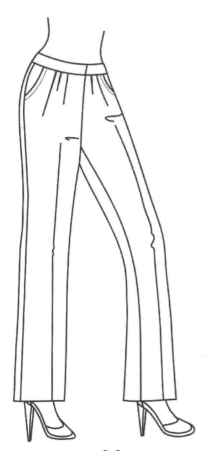

Pleated Front **X** This style can look mannish and shapeless unless worn with care. The area round the tummy is cut to give space around the tummy area and pocket area.

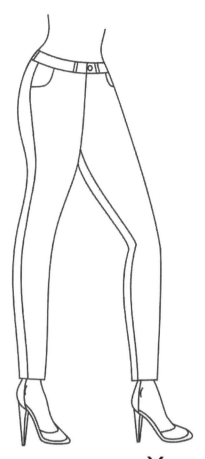

Tapered or "Skinny" **X** This style of trouser fits the legs, thighs and bottom very closely. It rarely works (unless you have model proportions) without a cleverly styled longer length top.

Copyrighted Material

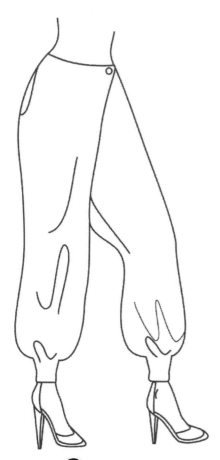

Harem **?** This style is a soft voluminous shape that disguises the appearance of thighs and bottom whatever your shape. A fitted waist is a must to create a flattering shape at the tummy. Hems are either cuffed or gathered anchoring the fabric round the leg, however, and will always place the focus on footwear.

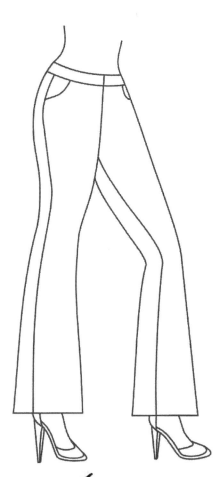

Bootleg ✔ This is a subtly flattering style that is wider at the bottom of the leg than the top. It will be fitted more closely to the thigh than the flared trousers and is a good general all rounder for any shape when styled with the right top.

Copyrighted Material

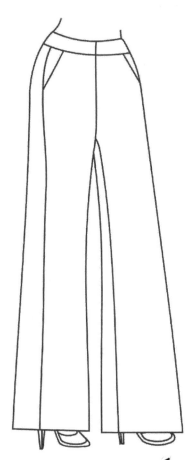

Palazzo or Wide Leg ✔ This is a wide, loose fitting style of trouser that usually appears in linen, cotton or other lightweight fabrics; heavier fabrics would be too stiff. Because of the width of this design it will create a foreshortening.

Copyrighted Material

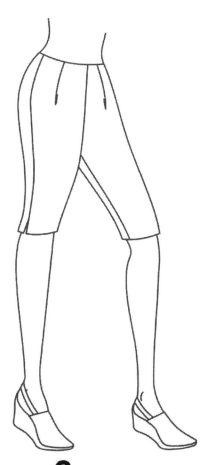

Capri **?** This style is fitted to the leg and cropped just above the calf. It will be free of too much detail as it needs to hug the body.

Shoes

Copyrighted Material

Pointed Toe ✔ The pointed toe is the style that offers the best tool to create a longer looking leg especially when worn as a court or sling back style as shown here. Remember to never wear in a color that matches your skin-- it will make your foot look enormous!

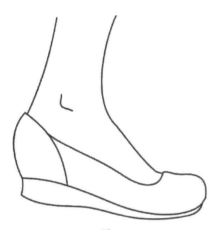

Round Toe ✔ The round toe is fashionable from time to time and when worn as a court style or sling-back style with no extra straps can look elegant on most legs. Prioritize this style if you have large feet, as this will make them look shorter.

Copyrighted Material

Strap Across Instep **?** Shoes like these can have any sized heel.
They appear practical and make great work shoes. It brings the
eye top the ankle and shortens the leg.

Ankle Strap **X** This style begins to shorten the leg and draw
attention to the calf, making it seem wider than it is. It also makes
the foot seem larger than it is if the design is flat at the heel.

Copyrighted Material

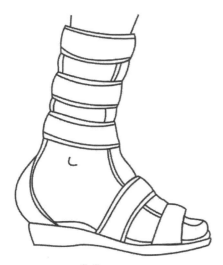

Gladiator **X** Any style of shoe that has straps travelling up the leg from the shoe can create a foreshortening effect on the leg to make it look wider and shorter.

Strappy Sandals **?** These can appear as a simple sandal style as illustrated here, but can look frivolous and fun so avoid in situations where you want to create some authority, like work.

Copyrighted Material

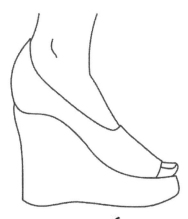

The Platform ✔ This style can sometimes appear as a small built up area of the sole or it can be a very large and chunky feature of the shoe. Choose a platform to balance your ankle and calf remembering that a thick, chunky shoe can make legs look more streamlined.

Peep Toe ✔ This is a universally flattering style because it helps to make all feet look smaller. It is also very adaptable for both formal and fun looks.

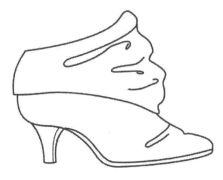

Low Ankle Boot **?** This style is usually worn with high fashion garments like pencil skirts and culottes.

High Ankle Boot **✔** These boots are perfect for a clean line under trousers and should never be worn with skirts or cropped trousers. Under long trousers they suit all body shapes.

Copyrighted Material

Shoe Boot **?** The shoe boot is a fashion style that has become popular and will foreshorten your leg if worn with a skirt. Try it with matching hosiery and skirt to get it looking right.

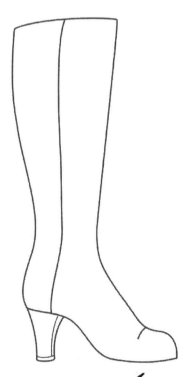

Fitted Knee High ✔ The fitted boot is a classic style and suit

Copyrighted Material

most legs and body shapes. This will be your most versatile buy and can work with a structured skirt, cropped trousers and jeans.

Mid Calf **X** Often mid calf boots give an urban and practical finish especially if they are flat but this calf length works just as well when it appears with a heel too. Look out because this boot cuts across the calf at its widest point and will add bulk to the leg.

Copyrighted Material

Knee High with Cuff **?** This style of boot in leather or suede can be worn over skinny jeans and trousers or under a skirt, which has some structure. The cuff works to widen the leg and but also shorten.

Accessories

Copyrighted Material

Structured Bag ✔ This is a bag that has a hard frame and looks perfect for more formal use like office or a special occasion. It comes in many colors and designs but it is the square corners that are the key part of the design.

Copyrighted Material

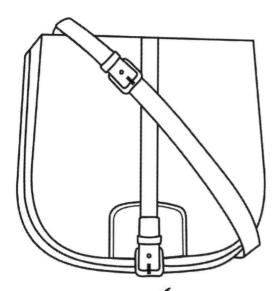

Saddlebag Style Bag ✔ This bag has more softness to it. It is usually in leather and needs a thought out approach. Make sure shoes or boots work with it because it is a dominant shape.

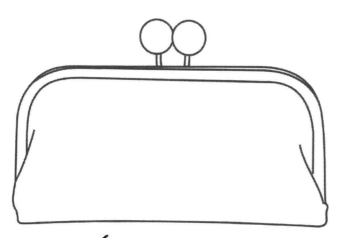

Clutch Bag ✔ If you are choosing an evening bag then the clutch is a great shape. Easy to hold, it has a flattering effect and can be eye catching by themselves because they are bright, shiny or jewel-like so match carefully to other accessories.

Copyrighted Material

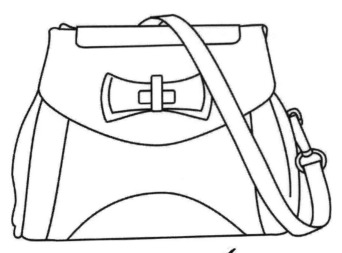

Softly Structured Bag with Flap ✔ This style of bag is less harsh than the structured bag style. It is more versatile for both occasion and office dressing, as well as more informal settings.

Pouch Bag ✗ This is a soft and squashy shape that can be

fabric, plain, patterned or leather. It has a fleshy feel to it and shouldn't be overstuffed. It can be very eye catching, and doesn't need to be matched to your shoes.

Bowling Bag Style **X** It often appears with extra pockets, flaps and side zips and has a young sporty feel.

Copyrighted Material

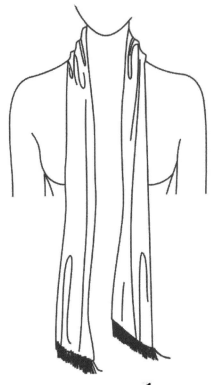

Long, Loose Scarf ✔ This scarf, when used as a contrasting color or pattern, will take the eye up and down the body to create vertical lines to elongate and streamline your upper body. It is an excellent device.

Copyrighted Material

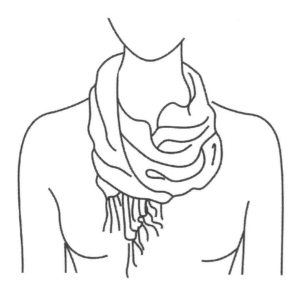

Long Wrap Around Scarf ✔ A scarf that is circled round the neck many times will make a neck look more slender and shoulders smaller.

Copyrighted Material

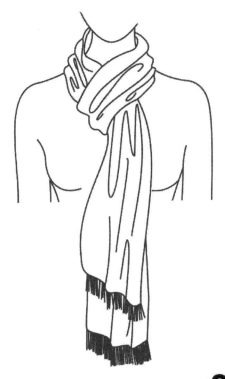

Long Loose and Looped Scarf **?** When a scarf is looped it draws the eye to wherever the loop is placed. It is a great device for adding volume at the chest and a useful foreshortening device if needed.

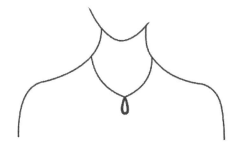

Necklace and Pendant at Neckline **X** Beware the necklace that does battle with the clothing neckline you have chosen; the two need to be separate. As a rule, delicate jewelry needs to be against the flesh whereas costume jewelry can look just as good against clothing.

Copyrighted Material

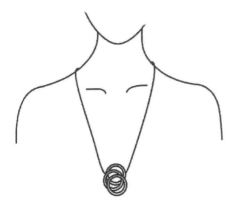

Drop Pendant **?** ▪ A longer pendant will always distort the length of the neckline and the upper torso. This style of pendant can make any plain top look very glamorous, but don't wear with busy top however.

Copyrighted Material

The Choker **X** This is a great piece of jewelry that gives slender necks some glamour and coverage. It can be worn with a high collar or just as well with a strapless gown.

Large Beads ✔ The larger you are, the larger your jewelry should be .This may be stating the obvious but a well balanced necklace will make your neck look more slender.

String of Chains **?** The overall effect here is to create an accessory look with more volume to flatter a lager or taller body.

Copyrighted Material

Large Pendant ✔ A large pendant looks stunning and will always help you to make a dramatic impact. To create the best effect, the size of the pendant should be in proportion with your body.

Epilogue

Thank you so very much for the opportunity to work with you on your new image, I like to think that as a result, you are well on your way to a lifelong love of clothes and of your body. Celebrate who you are and others will not be able to pinpoint the exact change in you, but they will notice your new found confidence and Zen for life. The secrets I have shared with you here will help you create a stylish and sophisticated exterior, but always remember that true beauty lies within.

Keep Smiling!

Isabella James

Stop by and visit at my fashion blog www.dressity.com

5412305R00074

Printed in Great Britain
by Amazon.co.uk, Ltd.,
Marston Gate.